# ALEJANDRO GARNACHO

## (The Future of Football)

*Biography Of Alejandro Garnacho*
*And What You Should Know About Him*

**Chris A. Dorton**

# Table Of Contents

## Alejandro Garnacho is a great footballer !

*(Alejandro Garnacho es un gran futbolista.)*

*(Alejandro Garnacho est un excellent footballeur.)*


## Alejandro Garnacho is the future of football!

*(Alejandro Garnacho es el futuro del fútbol)*

*(Alejandro Garnacho est l'avenir du football)*


## Do you believe it?

*( ¿lo crees)*

# INTRODUCTION

Manchester United, a club rich in history and culture, is located in the centre of Manchester, where football is more than simply a game. United, well-known for its ardent supporters and legendary players, has seen success and setbacks throughout the years, forming its identity.

Alejandro Garnacho, a young winger whose flare and tenacity have drawn the attention of both fans and commentators, is one of the most recent talents in Manchester United who grew from its academy.

The difficulties faced by young athletes in the cutthroat world of football are reflected in Garnacho's journey, which was filled with both opportunities and disappointments. His story is one of tenacity and drive as he deals with injuries and the demands of playing professionally.

This book explores the life of Alejandro Garnacho on the pitch and outside pitch. Garnacho's ascent is a ray of optimism for the team's future and his fans.

# Chapter 1: Who Is Alejandro Garnacho

Alejandro Garnacho is rapidly becoming known as one of the most promising young players in contemporary football. He epitomizes the football future at the young age of 19, captivating both fans and pundits with his unique combination of talent, speed, and creativity. He is currently regarded as an important member of his club and the Argentina national team after an incredible ascent through the ranks at Manchester United.

Garnacho's explosive style of play is what makes him unique. He is the type of winger who enjoys taking opponents one-on-one and generating scoring opportunities with his lightning-fast speed and close ball control. He adds a thrilling intensity to the field whether he's cutting inside to unleash a shot or racing down the flank. He is a flexible member of his squad who can adjust to different tactical configurations due to his ability to function well on both wings.

Garnacho's off-the-ball actions demonstrate his tactical knowledge in addition to his technical prowess. He can exploit openings and cause havoc in rival backlines because he is skilled at timing his runs and spotting gaps behind defenses. This talent for vertical play gives Manchester United's attack a much-needed dimension and aids in their ability to overcome obstinate defenses that have hampered them in previous campaigns.

Furthermore, Garnacho's talents go beyond simply scoring goals; he is also good at establishing midfield play. He is not only a flair player; he also recognizes the value of collaboration, as evidenced by his readiness to track back and assist defensive attempts. He will undoubtedly become an even more significant player as he continues to hone his physicality and decision-making skills.

Beyond his unique skills, Garnacho is significant because he embodies a new generation of young football players who are changing the modern definition of what it means to be a professional player. He stays grounded and concentrates on raising his game under the burden of expectations from both fans and commentators. Garnacho is positioned to become one of football's most notable stars as he continues to realize his full potential, motivating the upcoming generation of players and making a lasting impression on the game.

## Who is ALEJANDRO GARNACHO?

His first or paternal name is Garnacho, while his second or maternal family name is Ferreyra.
Born July 1, 2004, Alejandro Garnacho Ferreyra is a professional football player who plays winger for both the Argentina national team and Manchester United of the Premier League.

In October 2020, Garnacho moved from Atletico Madrid to Manchester United's youth academy. In May 2022, he was named the Jimmy Murphy Young Player of the Year and the FA Youth Cup winner. He made his first-team debut at the age of 17. Before earning his Argentina under-20 debut in 2022, Garnacho first competed his Spain's youth system, where he was born. He joined the squad that won the 2024 Copa América championship after making his debut for the senior Argentina squad in June 2023.

# Chapter 2: His Early Professional Life

## Manchester United

### Youth Career

Garnacho joined the Manchester United Academy in October 2020. Atlético was paid £420,000 by United. In July 2021, he agreed to his first professional contract with the team. Garnacho's solo goal in the FA Youth Cup victory over Everton garnered attention and was nominated for United's February 2022 Goal of the Month award.

Garnacho made his United first-team debut on April 28, taking Anthony Elanga's place in the 91st minute of a 1-1 draw with Chelsea, after being used as an unutilized replacement for multiple Premier League games. In May, Garnacho was named the Jimmy Murphy Young Player of the Year. He helped United win the FA

Youth Cup for the first time since 2011 by scoring twice against Nottingham Forest in the final on May 11.

**Season 2022–2023:**

He switched his shirt number from 75 to 49 for the 2022–2023 Premier League season. He scored a late goal for United's U-21 team against Barrow in the 2022–23 EFL. After making his first senior start for United on October 27 in a 3-0 victory over Sheriff Tiraspol of Moldova in the UEFA Europa League, manager Erik Ten Hag commended Garnacho for his growth over the previous few weeks, stating that while he had been previously unhappy, he was pleased with his increased resilience and attitude.

In Europa League game against Real Sociedad on November 3, he scored his first goal as a senior, assisted by his idol, Cristiano Ronaldo. On November 13, Garnacho scored the game-winning goal in injury time against Fulham, marking his Premier League debut.

Garnacho assisted Marcus Rashford in scoring the game-winning goal in the 82nd minute of the team's 2-1 victory over Manchester City on January 14, 2023, in the Manchester Derby.

Garnacho suffered ankle ligament damage during a match against Southampton on March 14 and declared he would be out for several weeks. Garnacho signed a new contract extension on April 28th, 2028, which will last until June 30th. After missing two months due to injury, Garnacho scored the second goal in a 2-0 victory over Wolves on May 13.

**Season 2023–2024**

Manchester United declared at the start of the 2023–24 Premier League season that Garnacho's squad number would be changed from 49 to 17. Garnacho scored in the 88th minute of a 3-1 loss against Arsenal on the road on September 3, but VAR controversially disallowed the goal for offside. United would have been ahead 2-1 if the goal had stood. In a 3–0 victory over Everton on

November 26, Garnacho opened the scoring with a bicycle kick from 15 yards (14 m) away, winning him the Premier League Goal of the Month award for November 2023 and ultimately the Premier League Goal of the Season.

Three days later, in a 3–3 way tie with Galatasaray, Garnacho scored his first Champions League goal. Garnacho scored two goals in a 3–2 comeback victory over Aston Villa on December 26. He scored two more goals in a 3-0 victory over West Ham United on February 4, 2024. He scored twice again on April 4, this time in a 4–3 loss to Chelsea on the road. This made him the first youngster since Michael Owen in 1998–1999 to score multiple braces in three Premier League games in a single season.

Garnacho opened the scoring in a 2-1 victory over Manchester City in the FA Cup final on May 25. In addition to becoming the second Argentinean to score after Ricardo Villa's brace for Tottenham Hotspur against City in 1981, his goal in the final was the first for a teenager since Cristiano Ronaldo in 2004.

## Season 2024–2025

Garnacho gave Manchester City the lead in the FA Community Shield on August 10, 2024. Even though Garnacho scored his penalty, United lost the shootout 7–6. The game ultimately finished in a 1–1 draw and went to penalties. He came on as a substitute and scored his first league goal of the season in a 3-0 victory over Southampton in an away match on September 14.

On September 17, he helped United defeat Barnsley 7–0 in the EFL Cup third round by scoring two goals and dishing out two assists. Garnacho made his 100th Manchester United appearance on October 27 2024 at London Stadium in a 2-1 loss to West Ham United.

# International Career

Because his mother is Argentine, Garnacho was qualified to play for both Argentina and Spain, where he was born. In 2021, he played three games for Spain's under-18 squad.

Garnacho was called up to the national Argentina squad on March 7, 2022, as part of the first 44-man roster for their two World Cup qualifying matches that month. Although he was included in the final 33-man roster for the fixtures, he did not play in either match.

On March 26, Garnacho began in a friendly match against the United States, marking his debut for the Argentina under-20 team. At the 2022 Maurice Revello Tournament, he won the Revelation Player and Goal of the Tournament titles after scoring four goals in four games for the under-20 squad.

He was called up to the national Argentina squad once again in March 2023 for two friendlies against Curaçao and Panama, however, he was forced to leave the camp due to an ankle injury. On June 15, he made his senior team debut at Workers' Stadium in a friendly match against Australia. He replaced Nicolás González in the second half of the match. Garnacho was part of Lionel Scaloni's final 26-man Argentina squad for the 2024 Copa América in June 2024, and the team went on to win the competition.

**Alejandro**
# GARNACHO
NOVEMBER    GOAL OF THE MONTH

# Chapter 3: Key Mentors and Coaches in Alejandro Garnacho's Development

Influential coaches and mentors who saw Alejandro Garnacho's potential and developed it have played a major role in his ascent through the football ranks. Key players in his growth include the following:

## Pérez, José Luis (Getafe CF Academy)

Garnacho was taught the basics of football at Getafe CF, where he started his football career. José Luis Pérez helped him acquire crucial abilities like positioning, ball control, and tactical awareness. Garnacho's comprehension of the game was shaped by Pérez's coaching, which also gave him a strong work ethic and a love for football.

## Ángel Rangel (Atletico Madrid Academy)

Garnacho joined Atletico Madrid's academy after his time at Getafe, where he was coached by Ángel Rangel. Rangel, who is renowned for emphasizing tactical discipline and technical talent, was instrumental in honing Garnacho's winging skills. In order to prepare Garnacho for competition at a higher level, his coaching concentrated on improving his dribbling, pace, and decision-making on the field.

## Nicky Butt (Manchester United Academy)

When Garnacho moved to Manchester United in 2020, Nicky Butt, who was then in charge of the academy, had a big impact on him. As a former United player, Butt was aware of the team's expectations and collaborated closely with Garnacho to develop his skills. Garnacho learned a lot from Butt about the mindset needed to be successful at a top team, which emphasized professionalism, perseverance, and the value of constant progress.

### Erik ten Hag (First Team Manchester United)

Under manager Erik ten Hag, Garnacho earned his first-team debut in the 2022–2023 campaign. Young players have been given opportunities in the senior group thanks in large part to the Dutch coach. Garnacho has been able to demonstrate his abilities on a bigger platform thanks to Ten Hag's tactical savvy and capacity to create a competitive atmosphere. Garnacho's growth as a player has been greatly aided by Ten Hag's faith and confidence in him, which has allowed him to express himself on the pitch and take chances.

### Cristiano Ronaldo (Training partner and idol)

Garnacho had the exceptional chance to train with one of the all-time greats, Cristiano Ronaldo, while he was at Manchester United. Garnacho has been greatly influenced by Ronaldo's professionalism, commitment, and work ethic. Garnacho has learned a great deal about upholding high standards on and off the field thanks to the opportunity to study under such an accomplished player.

# Chapter 4: Garnacho Compared With Other Young Footballers

Alejandro Garnacho, a young player with a lot of promise, is frequently compared to other up-and-coming players. Although he stands out due to his distinct playing style, strengths, and developmental trajectory, the competitive nature of this role is highlighted by his similarities to his contemporaries. Here is a closer look at Garnacho's standing with other prominent young players:

## Saka Bukayo (Arsenal)

Bukayo Saka, one of the most well-known young wingers in England, has had a big influence at Arsenal. Saka, who blends technical skills with tactical knowledge, is well-known for his remarkable dribbling, vision, and adaptability. Saka has a minor advantage in terms of experience and consistency at the senior level, even though Garnacho possesses the same flare and ability to take on defenders. Saka exhibits a level of maturity that Garnacho is still learning via his performances in high-stakes games, especially international competitions.

## Jude Bellingham (Real Madrid)

Jude Bellingham is one of the best young players in international football, even though he is now playing in La Liga. He is a special player because of his ability to control play from midfield and his potential to score goals. Both players have a great degree of technical skill and ball intelligence, even though Garnacho plays mostly as a winger.

Bellingham stands out due to his international tournament experience and early leadership abilities, but Garnacho is an exciting prospect in his own right because of his dynamic style and flare.

## Phil Foden (Manchester City)

Another exceptional young player who has performed well at Manchester City is Phil Foden. He is a versatile danger because of his technical skill, football IQ, and ability to play a variety of offensive positions. Similar to Garnacho, Foden can move through confined places with ease thanks to his rapid footwork and low center of gravity. But Garnacho still lacks the confidence and poise that Foden has because of his accomplishments, which include several Premier League titles and Champions League experience.

## Anthony Gordon (Newcastle United)

Another talented winger on the rise is Anthony Gordon, who has shown potential at Newcastle United. Like Garnacho, Gordon is renowned for his straightforward style of play and willingness to take on defenders. Both players have a talent for drawing fouls and are excellent one-on-one players. Garnacho is a more dynamic threat in transition, though, because of his speed and quick acceleration, which can help him break free from opponents.

**Harvey Elliott ( Liverpool)**

Another young player who is causing a stir in the Premier League is Harvey Elliott. He excels in a variety of offensive roles and frequently contributes to the build-up play thanks to his inventiveness and vision. Garnacho's style is more straightforward and explosive, whereas Elliott's is more concentrated on creating plays. Although both players have a ton of promise, Garnacho is a more dynamic threat in the final third due to his speed and ability to penetrate defenses.

**Cade Cowell (San Jose Earthquakes / USMNT)**

Cade Cowell is a dynamic young winger in Major League Soccer and a rising star in the U.S. men's national team, despite not playing in the Premier League at the moment. He is a player to monitor because of his unadulterated athleticism and ability to generate opportunities. Garnacho's technical skill and tactical awareness of the game distinguish him in a more subtle way than Cowell, whose style is slightly different due to his heavy reliance on physical qualities. Garnacho also has a tiny advantage in tactical awareness because of his background in a very competitive academy system.

## Cole Palmer (Chelsea)

Another young player coming out of Chelsea's ranks is Cole Palmer. Palmer is well known for his inventiveness and dribbling abilities, and in his few outings, he has displayed moments of genius. Palmer and Garnacho have similar qualities, such as the capacity to use imagination to alter games. In contrast to Palmer, who is still finding his niche, Garnacho has recently been handed a more prominent position in the first team, which has allowed him to solidify his place in the Premier League spotlight.

## Nicolas Jackson (Chelsea)

Despite being a forward by trade, Nicolas Jackson has shown great promise and has been used on the wing for Chelsea. He is notable for his speed and ability to penetrate defenses. Garnacho and Jackson are comparable, especially in their propensity to run behind the defense and their quickness. Nonetheless, Garnacho has an advantage in generating opportunities for himself and his teammates due to his technical proficiency and quick direction changes.

# Chapter 5: Garnacho's Notable Football Injuries And Net worth

## Football Injuries

Throughout his career, Alejandro Garnacho has sustained several significant injuries that have hindered his growth and playing time.

**Ankle Injury (March 2023):** Garnacho was forced to miss several weeks of action for the Argentina national team due to an ankle injury he sustained during a tackle in a match against Southampton.

**Knee Issues (October 2023):** He suffered from knee issues that caused him to be left out of the Argentina squad once more, which had an impact on his Manchester United performance at a pivotal time.

As he continues to make a name for himself in professional football, these failures have put his fortitude to the test while also offering him chances to develop.

## **Net Worth**

Alejandro Garnacho received a weekly salary of £50,000 in 2024, which translated into an annual income of £2.6 million from his Manchester United deal. He signed a contract with the club in April 2023 that will keep him there until June 2028, guaranteeing his financial stability for the foreseeable future. He is expected to make a total of £10.4 million over the four years left on his contract.

He is one of Manchester United's young, talented players earning this wage. Garnacho is only 20 years old, yet his salary is commensurate with his importance to the team.
He still has room to improve in comparison to other Premier League players. Nevertheless, his

steady performance guarantees that he will probably receive more pay raises and contract extensions.

His salary and endorsement agreements with companies like Nike are included in his total earnings, which further increases his yearly revenue. Alejandro Garnacho's wages will rise dramatically in the upcoming years due to his quick ascent and expanding reputation both on and off the field.

# Chapter 6: Garnacho's Private LIfe

Garnacho's identity is significantly shaped by his mixed heritage. Because his mother, Patricia, is from Argentina and his father, Alex, is Spanish, he was able to represent Argentina internationally, which strengthened his ties to his heritage.

## Family life

Garnacho was raised in a close-knit household. He has received constant support from his parents, who have helped him navigate the demanding world of professional football. Despite his growing celebrity, his mother in particular was crucial in teaching him self-control and humility. He is quite close to his brother, Roberto, who is his younger brother. Although their connection is still private, Garnacho has talked about how important family is to keep him grounded on occasion.

In his personal life, Garnacho is devoted to Eva García, his partner. The couple is quite close, and they have a baby boy named Enzo on October 4, 2023. For Garnacho, becoming a father at such an early age has changed his life. He frequently posts pictures of his family on social media, expressing his pride and affection for his partner and son. His posts show a gentler, more intimate side of him, whether he's sharing intimate moments or commemorating significant occasions.

## **Beyond Football**

Garnacho has a lifestyle that is typical of young football players off the field, but he adds his own special touch. As a fitness enthusiast, he frequently posts videos of his training and recuperation. Along with being a huge gamer, he has been seen playing FIFA and other well-known games with friends and teammates.

Garnacho is a tattoo enthusiast, and his ink frequently provoked discussion among followers. His journey, family, and passions are reflected in several of his tattoos, which have personal significance. Garnacho has also shown an interest in fashion, despite his youth. His outspoken demeanor on the field is in line with his sense of style, which combines high fashion with streetwear. He has become a trendsetter among younger players and fans as a result.

## Personality

Garnacho, who is described by teammates as self-assured and ambitious, strikes a balance between his fierce temperament on the field and his more relaxed manner off it. His family is a major part of his life away from football, and he attributes this to them helping to keep him grounded in the face of the demands of professional athletics.

In appreciation to his mother's ancestry, Garnacho has acknowledged in interviews his enjoyment of the small things in life, such as traveling, spending time with his loved ones, and eating Argentine food. His choice to play for the Argentina national team, where he is rapidly winning over supporters, is another indication of his dedication to his heritage.

# Chapter 7: Garnacho's Playstyle And Potential

## Garnacho's Playstyle

On the field, Alejandro Garnacho is a welcome change. His play is all about flair and pace. Garnacho is a youthful talent who can swoop past opponents as if they were motionless. With the ball stuck to his feet, he can dribble with amazing skill, swerving in and out of confined areas. His fearlessness is what truly makes him unique.

He loves to demonstrate his abilities and isn't afraid to take on defenders one-on-one. He frequently cuts in from the wing in an attempt to set up a teammate or take a shot. He has a talent for surprising everyone by making well-timed dashes behind the defense.

A little of that joyful swagger is also present in Garnacho; you can tell he's having fun out there because he plays with a smile on his face. He's still working on making better decisions in the last third, but when he does, it's magical. Watching him play is always thrilling, whether it's a brisk dash down the flank or a sly nutmeg. As he advances in his career, he's undoubtedly someone to watch!

Garnacho is a dynamic forward who has received recognition for his quickness and dribbling skills as well as his ability to generate opportunities and enter the box. He is regarded as one of Manchester United's academy's most promising talents. He has often been used as a winger on the left or right flank at United. He was called "everything that Manchester United is about" and "an intelligent player who understands his role in the team" by United coach Mike Phelan.

He idolises former Manchester United colleague, Cristiano Ronaldo, whose style of play has greatly impacted his own. When he scores a goal, he usually does Ronaldo's famous goal celebration style.

## Alejandro Garnacho Potential

The sky is Garnacho's starting point. He has been dominating with the U18s in addition to being promoted to the U23s. Alejandro Garnacho has already contributed significantly, especially in the FA Youth Cup. Last year, Garnacho and other fantastic young players like Kobbie Mainoo helped United win the competition after it had been lost for eleven years.

There was already a bustle around Garnacho. Because of his efforts and the triumph of the FA Youth Cup, it wasn't overflowing. Playing him will grow more appealing even though he hasn't yet made a name for himself in the senior system. Garnacho will undoubtedly follow suit and shortly join the team. Garnacho's route has never been more obvious because of his versatile style and shaky attack.

# Chapter 8: His Awards And Stats

## Garnacho's Awards

### Manchester United U18
- FA Youth Cup: 2021–22

### Manchester United
- FA Cup: 2023–24
- EFL Cup: 2022–23

### Argentina
- Copa América: 2024

### Individual

- Premier League Goal of the Season: 2023–24.
- Premier League Goal of the Month: November 2023.
- Jimmy Murphy Young Player of the Year: 2021–22

- Maurice Revello Tournament Revelation Player: 2022.
- Maurice Revello Tournament Best XI: 2022.
- Maurice Revello Tournament Goal of the Tournament: 2022.
- IFFHS Men's World Youth (U20) Team: 2023.
- BBC Goal of the Season: 2023–24.
- Manchester United Goal of the Season: 2023–24 (vs. Everton, 26 November 2023).

## Alejandro Garnacho's Form and Stats

With 15 goals and six assists in 32 games across all age levels in 2021–2022, Garnacho led the academy in scoring. In 12 Premier League 2 games, he assisted on one goal and scored four. Furthermore, the way that goal contributions occur is just as important as their quantity.

As Alejandro Garnacho shines in several categories, the crowd is ecstatic. He has scored from tremendous long-range goals, captivating single runs, set pieces, and more. He is a prime example of an all-around talent that will only become better with time. Garnacho has already lit up Old Trafford, even though he has played most of his games at Carrington.

In his two FA Youth Cup matches against Everton and Scunthorpe, he scored once each, including a Gareth Bale goal against the latter.

# Chapter 9: Interesting Facts About Garnacho

As an emerging star in the football world, Alejandro Garnacho is renowned for his skill and promise on the field. *How much do you do Garnacho, the wonder boy of Manchester United?*

## Individual History

1. Alejandro Garnacho Ferreyra is his full name.

2. Birthdate: July 1, 2004.

3. Birthplace: Madrid, Spain.

4. Dual nationality: Argentinian and Spanish.

5. Height: 1.8 metres (5 feet 11 inches).

6. Family History: His mother is Argentine, while his father is Spanish.

7. Siblings: Roberto is his younger brother.

8. Early Life: His job choice was influenced by his upbringing in a football-loving household.

9. Childhood Hero: One of his greatest inspirations is Cristiano Ronaldo.

10. Personal Life: He and Eva García are together, and on October 4, 2023, their son Enzo was born.

## Development of a Football Career

11. Youth Clubs: Before joining Manchester United, he played for Atletico Madrid.

12. Joining Manchester United: In October 2020, he was transferred to United's youth system.

13. Debut Year: On April 28, 2022, he made his Manchester United first-team debut.

14. Position: Can play as a forward but mostly plays as a winger.

15. Playing Style: Well-known for his quickness, dribbling prowess, and capacity to set up goals.

## Successes

16. FA Youth Cup Winner: Manchester United won the FA Youth Cup in May 2022.

17. Jimmy Murphy Young Player of the Year: Given this title in May 2022 in recognition of his youth team accomplishments.

18. First Senior Goal: On May 13, 2023, he scored his first senior goal for Manchester United.

19. International Debut: On June 15, 2023, he made his senior Argentina debut.

20. Copa América Champion: A member of the 2024 Copa América winning Argentina team.

## Highlights of the Performance

21. First Premier League Goal: Against Southampton on September 14, 2024, he scored his first league goal.

22. EFL Cup Performance: Against Barnsley on September 17, 2024, I scored two goals and disheveled two assists.

23. Community Shield Performance: On August 10, 2024, I scored in the FA Community Shield match against Manchester City.

24. Notable Games: Contributed significantly to several Manchester United games with significant stakes.

## Acknowledgment and Impact

25. Media Attention: At an early age, he received a lot of media attention for his performances.

26. Social Media Presence: He interacts with fans on social media sites.

27. Endorsements: Has agreements with well-known companies like Nike for endorsements.

## Aspects of Finance

28. Net Worth (2024): Approximately $1 million is estimated.

29. Weekly Salary (2024): Manchester United pays him about £50,000 a week.

30. Annual Salary (2024): He makes around £2.6 million a year.

## Competencies and Qualities

31. Dribbling Ability: He is commended for engaging defenders in one-on-one play.

32. Crossing Proficiency: Well-known for making precise crosses into the box.

33. Work Ethic: Acknowledged for his commitment to honing his craft and training.

## **Prospects for the Future**

34. Career Projection: regarded as one of football's most promising young players at the moment.

35. Manchester United deal Duration: He has a deal with the team that expires in June 2028.

## **Community Participation**

36. Charity Work: Participated in a range of philanthropic endeavors via Manchester United's neighborhood projects.

## Cultural Influence

37. Impact on Young Players: Garnacho is an inspiration to a lot of young football players around the world.

## Fun facts

38. Favorite Food: Loves asado (barbecue), a classic Argentine dish.

39. Interests Outside of Football: Likes to play video games and spend time with family.